Leaving Saturn

WINNER OF THE 2000 CAVE CANEM POETRY PRIZE

*Founded in 1996 by Toi Derricotte and Cornelius Eady,
Cave Canem is a workshop/retreat for African American poets
and is dedicated to nurturing and celebrating African American
culture. Cave Canem sponsors a poetry prize for the best original
manuscript by an African American poet who has not yet been
professionally published.*

✳

Frost Place 2004

Leaving Saturn

Poems by Major Jackson

THE UNIVERSITY OF GEORGIA PRESS

ATHENS AND LONDON

To Allen:

Admiration
+
Hope
for
Our Words.
Great meeting you!

Major

Published by the University of Georgia Press
Athens, Georgia 30602
© 2002 by Major Jackson
All rights reserved
Designed by Betty Palmer McDaniel
Set in 10 on 14 Minion by Bookcomp, Inc.
Printed and bound by McNaughton and Gunn, Inc.
The paper in this book meets the guidelines for
permanence and durability of the Committee on
Production Guidelines for Book Longevity of the
Council on Library Resources.

Printed in the United States of America
06 05 04 03   P 5 4 3

Library of Congress Cataloging-in-Publication Data
Jackson, Major, 1968–
Leaving Saturn : poems / by Major Jackson.
p. cm.
"Winner of the 2000 Cave Canem Poetry Prize"—P.
ISBN 0-8203-2342-X (pbk.: alk. paper)
1. African Americans—Poetry.   I. Title
PS3610.A354 L4 2002
811'.6—dc21   2001043072

British Library Cataloging-in-Publication Data available

for Langston & Anastasia

Contents

Foreword

AL YOUNG

African American musical and performing arts genius Sun Ra, composer of the songs "Space Is the Place" and "It's after the End of the World," claimed to have been sent from Saturn by higher powers. Echoing Sun Ra, Major Jackson writes in "Leaving Saturn"

> Mars is dying, it's after
> The end of the world.
> So here I am,
> In Philadelphia,
>
> Death's headquarters,
> Here to save the cosmos,
> Here to dance in a bed
> Of living gravestones.

In this, his sweet and bittersweet debut album of a book, Major Jackson tries out his many wings and voices. Understanding, as poet Michael S. Harper pointed out again and again, that history is your own heartbeat, Jackson embraces his own personal history and—braiding it with the complex history of his family, his friends, his communities, his city, his country, his civilization and imagination—he whispers and groans all the highlights to us, his umbilicus, in the primal language we still share.

Poetry, always the primal human language, went through a worrying transformation in eighteenth-century Europe at around the time the Industrial Revolution was getting off the ground. Romanticism was rearing its head of powdered wigs and readjusting its fussy duds while families broke up and farmers and other country folk drifted into the towns and cities. Up until then, poetry had always dealt with every subject under the sun and moon. Poetry taught, instructed, chronicled, reported, spoofed, and laid out matters of spirit, the world, the devil, and the flesh in language so lean, melodic, and rhythmic that lessons and whole lectures could be memorized agreeably by a largely unlettered populace.

But the romantic movement changed all of that. It was under the sway of this new, ego-centered thinking that poetry began to focus on the private, subjective *me*. Variations of "I do this, and I do that," or "I think this, and I think that" ran other poem-voices out of town. The "I" reigned and soon came to characterize all of poetry's cares and concerns. Hadn't the seventeenth-century French philosopher René Descartes already stated, "*Cogito ergo sum* (I think therefore I am)"? A century and a half later, England would practically invent the Industrial Revolution, and so it was the English Romantic poets (Byron, Coleridge, Wordsworth, Percy and Mary Shelley) who would personalize this viewpoint dramatically, then take it all the way out to sea, to the very edge of the world. Brilliantly, Mary Shelley, at age eighteen, sniffed which way the winds of technology were blowing. She captured its worrying drift in her 1818 novel, *Frankenstein*, whose message and the issues it raised are still as fresh as today's biotech stock profiles.

By the time colonialism, that reckless handmaiden of industrialism, crossed the seas, extracting from the traffic of refined sugar, tobacco, rum, coffee, tea, and slaves the kinds of staggering profits that CIA- and KGB-backed drug cartels and empires would later stash away in the twentieth century, everything was up for grabs. Nature, long believed by traditional peoples to be inseparable from human beings, was suddenly viewed merely as a base, a source of raw materials. Capital begot capitalism, which only seems to last as long as its sources of cheap labor and resources. In other words, to hold up the totem pole of ever-expanding profits, there has to be a "nigger" at the bottom.

The looting of distant lands went hand in hand with the African slave trade. As Europe grew rich, she turned riotous. Ancient monarchies wobbled from defeats at the hands of self-appointed romantics like Napoleon, under whose rule tyranny was legitimized. Almost a century later, the Bolsheviks would murder the Russian czar. Taking their cue from the Russian Revolution of 1917, Mussolini and Hitler—both socialists, both dictators—fashioned the economic system they called fascism. It is an overriding tenet of fascism that countries be run with the logic and efficiency of Big Business or, as we now proudly designate them, corporations. By the close of the twentieth century, the United States, Europe's triumphant savior, had become the most powerful corporate democracy (or "stockocracy") on earth.

So what has all of this got to do with this book you now hold in your hands, Major Jackson's *Leaving Saturn*? Absolutely everything. When, in his lead poem, "Urban Renewal," Jackson speaks of how "Penn's GREENE COUNTRIE TOWNE uncurled a shadow in the 19TH century / that descended over gridiron streets like a black shroud," the whole tone of this remarkable collection is sounded:

> The city breathed an incurable lung (TB in that time), trolleys
> clanged the day's despair. Workers in cotton mills and foundries
> shook heads in disbelief, the unfolding theme caked on ashen faces.

As that theme unfolds in American life with the speed of an instant replay, the meaning of Philadelphia's and all the rest of the republic's flickering history is captured as only a poet can capture whole moments and epochs in the turn of a phrase or a line:

> Democracy depends upon such literacy.
> Snapshots. Maps. The vendor's fist of stars and stripes—
> *She sewed pennants.* The public gallery of bronze statues
> whose Generals grimace frightened looks
> at the darkening scenery....
> Break beats blasting your limbs to Market,
> you're ghostbloom in the camera's flash,
> so they call you FURIOUS ROCKER, CRAZYLEGS,—

Winner of the Cave Canem Award, *Leaving Saturn* steers clear of the slavish and almost always predictable conventions of first collections by American poets. Jackson faithfully celebrates and winces at the usual rites of passage in poems like "Rock the Body Body":

At 10, I did THE FREAK with Nikki Keys
In a stairway at the Blumberg Housing Projects
As the music came to us on the 18th floor
Like the need for language or the slow passing
Of jets. A dare, we were up close, all pelvis
Taking in measured breaths before going down
Like a pair of park pigeons. We could have crushed
pebbles, thrown fine specks of dust
At the moon. . . .

However, Jackson also deals surprises, as in these lines from "The Pantomime":

I can't help but think of Larry

Who wrote "Love-me-tender"
    On his hand to the girl
        Of our dreams, who wore
    His mother's hats like Princess

Diana, who thought Kenny
    A heartthrob & once reached
        For Earl's wrist a muggy
    Night in July. With a terror

That stills me like a trophy,
    You stomp, kick as if rustling
        Autumn leaves. The heap
    Of colors flutter in my mouth

Like vowels. . . .

The taste of colors—blue-in-green, Martian red, the sun-bleached white of a Yoruba priest or priestess's gown—brightens these pages with life, with beauty and quality of strength that comes of loving the very world with which you must continuously do battle. With their thoughtful, wide-ranging lyricism, the poems in this first book by Major Jackson break down mental alleyways and allow us to "escape our own carcasses." Reading them, we become

> the wind, the stars, oceans
> Inhabiting a space reserved for ancestors.
> Locked in a rhythm of motion,
>
> Catching up with time, running alongside
> Our forefathers. . . .

For thousands of years the Dogon people of Mali have worshipped the barely visible star contemporary astronomers have named Sirius B, which revolves in an elliptical orbit around the somewhat more visible Sirius. When the celebrity astronomer Carl Sagan learned of this, he stated at once that surely some westerner at one time or another must have visited the Dogon and told them about this star. However, the Dogon have always been secretive about their knowledge of Sirius B, whose every feature and change they follow closely. Moreover, Dogon knowledge of Sirius B coincides with every new finding by modern astrophysicists. Pressed to tell how they know these things, the Dogon inevitably assert that their ancestors came from that star. Egyptian lore corroborates this ancient Dogon knowledge of extraterrestrial developments and beliefs, which, incidentally, the Dogon continue to transmit to their priesthood in the everlasting language of poetry. With fluency and feeling, Major Jackson speaks and plays this timeless tongue.

Acknowledgments

To the editors of the following publications where some of the poems in this collection—some of which have been revised—first appeared, I extend grateful acknowledgment:

American Poetry Review: "Leaving Saturn"
Boulevard: "Mr. Pate's Barbershop"
Callaloo: "Some Kind of Crazy," "Don Pullen at The Zanzibar Blue Jazz Cafe," "Pest"
Code: The Style Magazine for Men of Color: "Night Museum"
Crab Orchard Review: "Block Party," "Oregon Boogie"
Obsidian II: Black Literature in Review: "Blunts," "A Joyful Noise"
New Yorker: "Euphoria," "How to Listen"
Painted Bride Quarterly: "Rock the Body Body"
Philadelphia Inquirer: "Mr. Pate's Barbershop"
Post Road: "Indian Song," "Urban Renewal IX"
Xavier Review: "Born under Punches"
"Euphoria" appears in *Reading & Writing the Human Experience,* edited by Richard Abcarian and Marvin Klotz and published by Bedford/St. Martin's Press, 2001.
"Some Kind of Crazy" appears in *Beacon's Best of 1999: Creative Writing by Men & Women of All Colors,* edited by Ntozake Shange and published by Beacon Press, 1999.
"Don Pullen at The Zanzibar Blue Jazz Cafe," "Some Kind of Crazy," and "Blunts" appear in *Spirit & Flame: Anthology of Contemporary African American Poetry,* edited by Keith Gilyard and published by Syracuse University Press, 1997.
"Don Pullen at The Zanzibar Blue Jazz Cafe" and "A Lesson after Swimming" appear in *Xconnect: Writers of the Information Age,* edited by David Edward Deifer and published by CrossConnect, Inc., 1996.

"Duck Girl on the Occasion of Spring" was commissioned and performed by Concerto Soloists Chamber Orchestra in November 1996 at Holy Trinity Church (Philadelphia) with music composed by David Saturen and photography by Frank Leone.

"Urban Renewal" was commissioned as one of seven segments featured in "Words in Place," a poetry video presentation directed by Glenn Holsten that aired on WHYY-TV12 (PBS-Philadelphia).

A warm and special thanks is also extended to Toi Derricotte, Cornelius Eady, Garrett Hongo, Kristen Johanson, Dorianne Laux, Joe Millar, Sonia Sanchez, Pimone Triplett, Reetika Vazirani, Afaa M. Weaver, Cave Canem, The Dark Room Collective (especially Thomas Sayers Ellis, Sharan Strange, Natasha Trethewey, and Artress Bethany White), Fine Arts Work Center in Provincetown, The Painted Bride Art Center, The Pew Charitable Trusts, The Mac-Dowell Colony, and Xavier University of Louisiana for vital resources in completing this collection.

Much of this book would not have been written without the support and care of family and friends including: Wadud Ahmad, Jose Chaves, Jennifer Donnelly, Willa Mae Duncan, Major Gooch, Marquita Mack, Noel D. Matthews II, Lavorn G. Spann, Rochelle Vassell, Janet Zweig, and many, many more.

Part One

*

Urban Renewal

i. Night Museum

By lamplight my steady hand brushes a canvas—
faint arcs of swallows flapping over rooftops
swiftly fly into view, and a radiant backdrop
of veined lilac dwindling to a dazzling cerise
evokes that lost summer dusk I watched
a mother straddle a stoop of brushes, combs,
a jar of ROYAL CROWN. She was fingering rows
dark as alleys on a young girl's head cocked
to one side like a MODIGLIANI. I pledged
my life right then to braiding her lines to mine,
to anointing streets I love with all my mind's wit.
The boy in me perched on the curb of this page
calls back between blue-sky Popsicle licks
that festive night the whole block sat out
on rooftops, in doorways, on the hoods of cars;
a speaker blared STEVIE above BULLOCK'S CORNER STORE
awash in fluorescence as the buoyant shouts
of children sugared a wall of hide-and-seek.
Because some patron, fearing she's stumbled
into the wrong part of town, will likely clutch
her purse and quicken pace, I funnel all the light
spreading across that young girl's lustrous head
with hopes we will lift our downturned eyes,
stroll more leisurely, pour over these sights.

ii.

Penn's GREEN COUNTRIE TOWNE uncurled a shadow in the 19TH
   century
that descended over gridiron streets like a black shroud
and darkened parlors with the predatory fog of prosperity
as familiar as the ornate plot in a Dickens novel.
The city breathed an incurable lung (TB in that time), trolleys
clanged the day's despair. Workers in cotton mills and foundries
shook heads in disbelief, the unfolding theme caked on ashen faces.
Above mantels in gilded frames: tasseled carriages, silk bonnets,
linen parasols echoing the silence of Victorian evil,
the shade soldered to new empires as steam engines hissed,
and brought this century's opening chapter to a creeping halt.
Step on a platform in our time, the city's a Parthenon,
a ruin that makes great literature of ghostly houses
whose hulking skin is the enduring chill of the western wind.
Stare back down cobbled alleys that coil with clopping horses,
wrought-iron railings, to grand boulevards that make a fiction
of suffering; then stroll these crumbling blocks, housing projects,
man-high weeds snagging the barren pages of our vacant lots.

iii.

You are almost invisible in all this plain decay.
Children's laughter echoing in arcs of hydrant water–spray
knots the heart; those black bathers like Cézannes
will soon petrify to silence. A chorus of power lines
hums a melancholic hymn, tenements' aching pyrrhics,
doorways and row-homes crumbling to gutted relics:
this one exposing a nude staircase, that one
a second-floor ceiling where swings
a lightbulb like your chipped soul suspended
from a thread of nerves. You have never imagined
a paradise, nor made a country of your ghetto,
only suffered the casket a vessel for the human shadow,
only feared, longing for other stones to worship.
Sun dreams the crowns of trees behind skyscrapers.
Here the heart is its own light; a pigeon's gurgle
sings the earth. The eyes of the dead float around us: muraled
Polaroids, street-corner billboards whose slogans
read, *"Aching humans. Prosperous gardens."*

iv.

From the LIBERTY BELL's glass asylum,
tourists emerge convinced of a cracked republic,
and for signs further join the edge of the human
circle where you break-dance the bionic two-step.
Democracy depends upon such literacy.
Snapshots. Maps. The vendor's fist of stars and stripes—
She sewed pennants. The public gallery of bronze statues
whose Generals grimace frightened looks
at the darkening scenery. Your Kangoled head spins
on cardboard, a windmill garnering allegiance.
Here prayed those who signed for Independence.
Break beats blasting your limbs to Market,
you're ghostbloom in the camera's flash,
so they call you FURIOUS ROCKER, CRAZYLEGS,—
The circle tightens like a colony, horse-and-carriages
hemming OLDE CITY to scraps of time;
squirrels pretremble then leap to bark.
Tourists ease on shades to enhance the dark.

v. To Sonia Sanchez

When death arrived like a police chopper in Ray Bans,
and the paralyzed songs of children congealed
to blocks of coal in your throat, and fingernail
clippings of bankers flooded nightly your dreams,
you, seeing the future creep towards the past in a stutter,
coughed, "What of our tomorrows? the legacy of our
dreams?" Down Lombard, near the A.M.E.,
Du Bois's ward of PHILADELPHIA NEGROES, strutting
beneath ginkgo trees you told the story of the trip—
the People's Republic of China, '73, a swelling hunger
after a long flight, Mao's reception and the other
delegates, starving artists whose chopsticks
moved faster than their mouths. That evening,
famished in your room, you practiced with beads
from your earrings, air tasting soft as bread,—
later, Mao's patience, love for his people "flowering."
Sonia, I remember the color of the night;
faces gathered in communion on the walls,
orishas from the shore, the sax player's wailing,
COUSIN MARY's righteous third eye stretched
a garden of prayers, drums slashed through fields,
like the sticks you carried in your purse for years,
a reminder to journey through the circle
of tongues, your screams blooming to a wail.

vi. To Sonia Sanchez II & Chinua Achebe

Lollygagging beneath the bell tower at TEMPLE,
I, sidling up to a girl for the weekend,
saw you cross the campus . . . my spine straightened—
"Come, young brother, to Bard, to the Catskills.
Come sing your poems on the Hudson."
The smoky outline of Jersey's industrial turnpike lights
shone like lost stars dim. Shawled in a limousine,
you hummed and swayed to Ellington,
and I thought of the profane shadows of ancestors
who rumbled north through foliated darkness and the air
they rode to flesh our bones, Ibo-fresh, and their cool stare,
which now entranced the night. Seeing me chatter
with history's tinted saints, you moaned a language
of rivers, of cathedrals, boxelders and pines, the skin
we pressed our bodies into when hounds trailed close as sin,
when hummingbirds entered the heart as if caged
by their own sweet will, and I listened to the birth
of a forest that grew deep in my ribs, the wet thickets
of blackberry tangle, bracken and motes of gnats,
bramble snapped and mossed over like some tattered
blanket of a lesser god. Dispossessed at water's edge
by rhythm's purified time, by a deeper knowledge,
something migratory and angular, I washed
by a half-moon my lips equipped for war.
Again I swam the luxury of your eyes—
my totemic soul, iron-wrought, at the gate
of imperceptible relations, pulling the world.
When we arrived, earth seeped from his mouth—
the fragility of African genius, shrines of the Old South.

vii. Sunday in July

In the dry pit of picnic grills, a dusty stillness.
The laborious wheeze of afternoon slumber,
and overhead, flies in a holding pattern.
Passing clouds mime the faith of ushers, a beguiled
congregation swaying beneath the white-gloved hands
of heaven. Fan a preacher's one-day sale, chipped
-toed Jesus in the rear of a storefront church.
All burdens lay down, all sins suspended.
You've seen man's inner furnace scorch this city,
not like the driver who opened fire on a street corner
of children, nor the teen mother pushing her young
from a project roof, nor the husband who held his family
hostage, but the sharp sparks of cruelty that explode
off-the-cuff: in a urinous bed, an elderly woman curses
the caretaker who smacks her hourly with a flyswatter;
on a sidewalk, shirtless boys play a game of dozens,
and soon a sucker punch, the wrong word about
someone's mother. In a beat, jam-packed bus,
the poor return in their Sunday best, breaking a sweat;
windows open, they haven't a chance. Hurry dusk!
All's combustible; streets flare up and the slid
-ing window of an ice-cream truck opens like the gospel.

viii. Block Party

[FOR THE ROOTS]

Woofers stacked to pillars made a disco of a city block.
Turn these rhymes down a notch and you can hear
the child in me reverb on that sidewalk where
a microphone mushroomed with a Caliban's cipher.
Those couplets could rock a party from here to Jamaica.
Its code was simple: *Prospero's a sucker-emcee.*
Smoke rising off a grill threatens to cloud all memory;
my only light, the mountainous cones of street lamps.
Did not that summer crowd bounce in ceremonial fits?
Ah yes! It was the deejay, and his spinning TECHNICS
delicately needled a groove, something from James Brown's
FUNKY PRESIDENT. Then, working the cross-fade
like a light switch, he composed a stream of scratches,
riffs. Song broken down to a dream of song flows
from my pen; the measured freedom coming off this page
was his pillared spell of drums—it kept the peace.
A police car idled indifferently at the other end of the street.
What amount of love can express enough gratitude
for those reformulations, life ruptured then looped back,
def and gaudy like those *phat,* gold chains?
Keep to sampling language, keep it booming
like Caliban yelling, *Somebody! Anybody! Scream!*

ix. To Afaa M. Weaver

Bless your hallowed hands, Sir, and their paternal blues.
Tonight Kala grazes a palm over a battered face,
feeling his newborn features in a Correctional zoo.
The shock is permanent like the caged primate
who suddenly detects he's human. A HOMO ERECTUS
stands upright on guard outside his cell.
For the record, good friend, tropes are brutal,
relentless, miraculous as a son's birth. KING KONG's
memoir gets repeated on the evening news
like a horror flick, and everywhere dark men
are savagely ambushed. So, when a woman strolls
towards a homeless BIGGER, the audience
tenses up involuntarily beneath a cone of light.
This is the work of blockbusters: Kala's groan
twisting on a steel cot, and by morning's sunlight,
your cramped hand. Pages pile to a tome
on a kitchen table; its defense is three-fifths
human, two-fifths man. I await its world premiere;
till then, when one hears of black guards who strike
harder, the brain goes arthritic, tropes proliferate,
and a wide screen blooms with images of heavyweights
whose gloved hands struggle to balance a pen.

x.

These murky streets run like streams, boulevards
widen to rivers, and your pen lifts like the blade of an oar
out of cement; one stroke and the brain tires—
On the tube, Fred Sanford rummaging the script,
on one toe, frenzied, maniacal, hand-grips
his heart for his muse, Elizabeth; all that wide-eyed dancing—
In the foyer, her robed, decadent silhouette.
The taxi driver pulls away, a barge
dreaming downstream. Upstairs the open bed
like a Kansas plain, yet the kitchen
sink serves your choosing. Impish fish,
you swim upstream and cling, the wake of hunger—
Skins drag; currents drench your tongue.
You row for reflection as every action has an equal,
the stamina of legends; rowing is vital.

xii.

North of Diamond Lake, the Cascades, crossmarks
of yew trees, calligraphic leafblades like credits,—
scrolling, behind the scenes, relegated,
we're lost and drive to a pass snow-blocked.
Listening to THIS AMERICAN LIFE,
the brute scoop broadcast as matter-of-fact,
our lives armed with tears in four acts:
Bonding's like scaling Kilimanjaro. Quite
naturally, love's whacked our ribs to steel,—
so, we're better off shoveling vignettes?
Imagine Auden dear penning antisonnets,
reasoning we've relinquished a good deal
of vocation. A frayed-winged hawk squawks
above in piercing kilowatts and anoints these summits
coolly with his feathered-blood. What's lost?
the kickback of Orpheus; his acoustics lack
confession, and still we turn and inch downhill
in narrow S's, guided by the compass
below his heart. Suffering in nature, the valley rising
on the backs of roadkill. Darling, how else
do we know we are here? These leaves
pinwheeling are songs I sing both grievous
and bracing; each groan puts us closer to the grave.

Part Two

*

Hoops

Trees fall so I can play
ground with my ink.
DE LA SOUL

I.

Bound by a falling CYCLONE
fence, a black rush streaks
for netless hoops, & one alone
from a distance, seeming to break

above the undulant pack, soars—
more like a Sunday SKYWALK,
he cups the ball, whirls his arm,
swoops down a TOMAHAWK.

Radar! Don't fly without me!
It's Big Earl who coughs, then downs
his bottle, a 40 oz. of OLDE E.
Laughter makes its rounds.

I cross a footpath of a city block,
a short rut that snakes between
a lush epitaph of dandelions
& weed-brush behind Happy

Hollow Courts; the ghost
of a staircase echoes here: sign
of lives lived, of souls lost.
Mottled hues of graffiti lines

bombed on this wall, PHASE
says DON'T STOP THE BODY ROCK.
At gate's entrance, my gaze
follows Radar & his half-cocked

jump shot. All morning I sang
hymns, yet weighed his form:
his flashing the lane,
quick-stop, then rise like popcorn.

Now, elbows set, a pair
of handlebars, he flicks his wrist,
the ball arcs through sunlight glare—
splashes the basket's

circle of air. A boom box bobs
& breaks beats on a buckling sea
of asphalt;—the hard,
pounding rhymes of BDP

flooding a wall as a crowd
of hustlers toss craps, waging
fists, dollar bets, only louder—
& one, more enraged,

promises to pistol-whip
the punk who doesn't pay.
Doubling down, he blows a kiss;
each dealer counts his days.

I turn from these highlights
as SPALDINGS fly like meteors.
Radar dribbles near. I'm late
& before I say a word:

Shootin' more geometry?
We laugh. Father Dave, coach
at St. Charles, once let me
play as a walk-on in hopes

I would tutor Radar. Not even
Pythagoras could awaken
in his head the elegance
of a triangle's circumference.

Four years later, he's off
on scholarship to UNC.
I'm to study Nabokov
at the state's university.

Proof of Pop-pop's maxim,
There's more ways to skin . . .
If the slum's our dungeon,
school's our Bethlehem.

Yet, what fate connects those dots
that rattle in hustler's palms
with Radar's stutter-step
& my pen's panopticon?

It casts shadows dark
as tar as we begin
a full-court run. A brick
off the half-moon's side

—in waves, we sprint.
No set offence: his pass,
my bounce, his eloquent
lateral two-hand jam.

Mr. Pate's Barbershop

I remember the room in which he held
a blade to my neck & scraped the dark
hairs foresting a jawline: stacks of Ebonys
& Jets, clippings of black boxers—
Joe Frazier, Jimmy Young, Jack Johnson—
the color television bolted to
a ceiling like the one I watched all night
in a waiting room at St. Joseph's
while my cousin recovered from gunshots.
I remember the old Coke machine, a water
fountain by the door, how I drank
the summer of '88 over & over from a paper
cone cup & still could not quench my thirst,
for this was the year funeral homes boomed,
the year Mr. Pate swept his own shop
for he had lost his best little helper Squeaky
to cross fire. He suffered like most barbers
suffered, quietly, his clippers humming so loud
he forgot Ali's lightning left jab, his love
for angles, for carpentry, for baseball. He forgot
everything & would never be the same.
I remember the way the blade gleamed
fierce in the fading light of dusk & a reflection
of myself panned inside the razor's edge
wondering if I could lay down my pen, close up
my ledgers & my journals, if I could undo
my tie & take up barbering where
months on end a child's head would darken
at my feet & bring with it the uncertainty
of tomorrow, or like Mr. Pate gathering

clumps of fallen hair, at the end of a day,
in short, delicate whisks as though
they were the fine findings of gold dust
he'd deposit in a jar & place on a shelf, only
to return Saturdays, collecting, as an antique dealer
collects, growing tired, but never forgetting
someone has to cherish these tiny little heads.

Euphoria

Late winter, sky darkening after school,
& groceries bought from Shop-Mart,
My mother leaves me parked on Diamond
To guard her Benz, her keys half-turned
So I can listen to the Quiet Storm
While she smokes a few white pebbles
At the house crumbling across the street.

I clamber to the steering wheel,
Undo my school tie, just as Luther Vandross
Starts in on that one word tune, "Creepin'."
The dashboard's panel of neon glows,
And a girl my age, maybe sixteen or so,
In a black miniskirt, her hair crimped
With glitter, squats down to pane glass,

And asks, *A date, baby? For five?*
Outside, street light washes the avenue
A cheap orange: garbage swirling
A vacant lot; a crew of boys slap-boxing
On the corner, throwing back large swills
Of malt; even the sidewalk teeming with addicts,
Their eyes spread thin as egg whites.

She crams the crushed bill down
Her stockings, cradles & slides her palm
In rhythm to my hips' thrashing,
In rhythm to Luther's voice, which flutters
Around that word I now mistake for "Weep"
As sirens blast the neighborhood &
My own incomprehensible joy to silence.

Out of the house my mother steps,
Returned from the ride of her life,
Studies pavement cracks for half-empty vials,
Then looks back at bricked-over windows
As though what else mattered—
A family, a dinner, a car, nothing
But this happiness so hard to come by.

Blunts

The first time I got high I stood in a circle
of boys at 23rd & Ridge tucked inside
a doorway that smelled of piss. It was
March, the cold rains all but blurred
our sight as we feigned sophistication
passing a bullet-shaped bottle of malt.
Johnny Cash had a love for transcendental
numbers & explained between puffs resembling
little gasps of air the link to all creation was
the mathematician. Malik, the smartest
of the crew, counterargued & cited the holy life
of prayer as a gateway to the Islamic faith
that was for all intents the true path
for the righteous black man. No one disputed.
Malik cocked his head, pinched
the joint & pulled so hard we imagined
his lips crazy-glued into stiff O's. It was long
agreed that Lefty would inherit his father's
used-car business, thus destined for a life of wrecks.
Then, amid a fit of coughing, I broke
the silence. *I want to be a poet.* It was nearing
dinnertime. Jësus lived here. His sister was yelling
at their siblings over the evening news & game shows.
The stench of hot dogs & sauerkraut drifted
down the dank hallway. A prespring wind flapped
the plastic covering of a junkman's shopping cart
as Eddie Hardrick licked left to right, the thin strip
of glue at the edge of a rolling paper, then uttered,
So, you want the tongue of God. I bent double
in the blade of smoke & looked up for help.
It was too late; we were tragically hip.

Born under Punches

The deejay fingered a 12"
From a batch of milk crates &
We were back inside the school
Gymnasium, catwalking between
Slowdrags & hipgrinds.

Skullcaps pulled below
Brows, Timberlands
Laced high, our fists swelled
Inside goosedown, metallic
Parkas. Spacemen

On the dance floor!
Heavy-eyed, feral-faced,
We roamed till some
Boy's neck flashed
Links of gold.

When Big Jake threw
A sucker punch, the boy
Fell like a swimmer
Given up breathing. Lovers
Left each other's arms,

Backing away.
Someone's sister moaned
In the bleachers &
A heavy groove
Unlocked a flurry of fists.

In that darkness,
Speakers rose like
Housing projects,
Moonlight diamonded
Mesh-wire panes.

What was it that bloomed
Around his curled
Body when the lights
Came up, fluorescent,
Vacant, garish?

The gym throbbed
With beats & rage
And his eyes darted
Like a man nailed
To a burning crucifix.

Wuxia

air was cut   severed
improvised like lightning   grunts

formed ten feet high   thrusts
of flesh   the stabbing of a million

molecules on a silver screen   we took
the hint   the way voices defied

symmetry with tongue   lip gestures
the whack of skin struck the eardrum

into fits of sweat and awe   chopsticks
blurred vision   demanded space in the dark

now you must die   we cheered as children
do when heads rolled like basketballs

coming to rest   outside we mimicked
combinations   elbow to knee

foot on neck ear in palm   landing
in a sea of popcorn   chewies

a sticky descent   the aching
build in us   like light

blasting our knuckles at anything
the craving to jump up   hover above

the universe like flames   frame by
frame   a continent of movements teased

the web of our world   with names
like centipede   toad   scorpion   snake

lizard we belonged to the family of venoms
poisoning   being poisoned by revenge

Some Kind of Crazy

It doesn't matter if you can't see
Steve's 1985 Corvette: Turquoise-colored,
Plush purple seats, gold-trimmed
Rims that make little stars in your eyes

As if the sun is kneeling, kissing
The edge of sanity. Like a Baptist
Preacher stroking the dark underside
Of God's wet tongue, he can make you

Believe. It's there, his scuffed wing-
Tips—ragged as a mop, shuffling
Concrete—could be ten-inch Firestone
Wheels, his vocal chords fake

An eight-cylinder engine that wags
Like a dog's tail as he shifts gears. Imagine
Steve, moonstruck, cool, turning right
Onto Ridge Avenue, arms forming

Arcs, his hands a set of stiff C's
Overthrowing each other's rule,
His lithe body and head snap back
Pushing a stick shift into fourth

Whizzing past Uncle Sam's Pawn
Shop, past Chung Phat's Stop & Go.
Only he knows his destination,
His limits. Can you see him? Imagine

Steve, moonstruck, cool, parallel,
Parking between a Pacer and a Pinto—
Obviously the most hip—backing up,
Head over right shoulder, one hand

Spinning as if polishing a dream;
And there's Tina, wanting to know
What makes a man tick, wanting
A one-way trip to the stars.

We, the faithful, never call
Him crazy, crackbrained, just a little
Touched. It's all he ever wants:
A car, a girl, a community of believers.

Pest

I heard the terrible laughter of termites
deep inside a spray-painted wall on Sharswood.
My first thought was that of Swiss cheese
hardening on a counter at the American Diner.
My second thought was that of the senator
from Delaware on the senate floor.
I was on my way to a life of bagging tiny mountains,
selling poetry on the corners of North Philly,
a burden to mothers & Christians.
Hearing it, too, the cop behind me shoved me
aside for he was an entomologist
in a former lifetime & knew the many
song structures of cicadas, bush crickets &
fruit flies. He knew the complex courtship
of bark beetles, how the male excavates
a nuptial chamber & buries himself—
his back end sticking out till a female sang
a lyric of such intensity he squirmed like a Quaker
& gave himself over to the quiet history
of trees & ontology. All this he said while
patting me down, slapping first my ribs, then
sliding his palms along the sad, dark shell
of my body.
                                    How lucky I was
spread-eagled at 13, discovering the ruinous cry
of insects as the night air flashed reds
& blues, as a lone voice chirped & cracked
over a radio; the city crumbling. We stood
a second longer sharing the deafening hum
of termites, back from their play & rest,
till he swung suddenly my right arm then my left.

The Pantomime

My best game ahead
   I dribble between my legs
      Down Master Street, criss-
Crossing like a pair

Of gleaming scissors—
   Precise & sharp. My bedazzled
      Opponents spin in my mind
Like awkward ice-skaters.

I stutter-step to the right,
   Fake left, carry the ball
      Round my back, in a flow
That speaks something

Of elegance & grace
   In the traffic of men.
      The finishing touch:
A fade-away jumpshot?

A finger-roll down the lane?
   No, I pull up top of the key
      Like Magic, slowly rising,
Air like boosters I gather

Round my knees for lift.
   I follow the arc my Spalding
      Makes, regal, a flaming
Ball of orange fire released

Over a steely sky, & find you,
  Captain of Franklin High
    Basketball team, screaming
  At a man, *Fuckin' Faggot!*

Frost of November air,
  Upper-cuts, overhand rights,
    Wind-beaters, a golden glove.
  I can't help but think of Larry

Who wrote "Love-me-tender"
  On his hand to the girl
    Of our dreams, who wore
  His mother's hats like Princess

Diana, who thought Kenny
  A heartthrob & once reached
    For Earl's wrist a muggy
  Night in July. With a terror

That stills me like a trophy,
  You stomp, kick as if rustling
    Autumn leaves. The heap
  Of colors flutter in my mouth

Like vowels. Tomorrow,
  You will appear on my stoop
    In your Adidas sweat suit &
  A basketball clutched under

Your arm, & ask, *Do I know*
   What it takes? I will punch
      The ball out of your grip,
      Pretend to race to the courts

Like a Laker's fast-break:
   One pass, then another
      & then a slam dunk
      To conceal my fear.

Rock the Body Body

for Cornelius Eady

I.

One summer night I learned the art of
Break dancing from a guy I'd only known
As Moon in exchange for algebra lessons
On Mondays. A member of the Pop-Along-Kids,
Moon taught me how to flick my wrist
& make a wave. "Check out The Electric
Boogie." he said & worked like a robot;—
One hand extended, the fingers curling &
Uncurling as the arm joints & shoulders, in one
Fluid motion, followed each other like butterflies.
I half-watched, trying to mimic the simple
Placement of feet, but mainly, I thought
Of all the girls that would soon form a circle
As I created illusions with my body.

II.

Mostly Saturdays, I would pass out
Of sight on the dance floor at Chestnut
& 13th beneath a vertiginous globe
Swirling as if each country were a beam
Of light. But nothing brought me closer
To the body politic than when I thrust
My arms out on rhythm & swung
My torso, pirouette-fashion, doing
THE CABBAGE PATCH! Half of what I knew
Of living I discovered in a disco:
The deft execution of bones,
Eyes, muscles, or something so basic
As keeping in step with your fellow man.

III.

You could be at a gay club with your girlfriend
Who insisted on your accompanying her
So that you might broaden your horizons
& be struck in awe at the elegance
Of movement in a dance you heard someone
Mention vaguely as VOGUING. The sight of men
Prancing about like royalty, stretching out
Limbs, pampering their features is enough
To inspire a frolicsome bone in your body & join
The fray. The beckoning voice of a man—
Work & work. Now turn & pose—is enough
For you to believe it's all a conspiracy. But you
Don't fight it. You like molding your face,
Twirling in a constellation of men.

IV.

At 10, I did THE FREAK with Nikki Keys
In a stairway at the Blumberg Housing Projects
As the music came to us on the 18th floor
Like the need for language or the slow passing
Of jets. A dare, we were up close, all pelvis
Taking in measured breaths before going down
Like a pair of park pigeons. We could have crushed
pebbles, thrown fine specks of dust
At the moon. We formed the precise motion
Of well-oiled gears fit to groove. This was three years
Before I would have sex for the first time,
Before I would discern the graceful tangle
Of stray gods, the bumbling dance of mortals.

Alleyways

We called them Brigantine Castles,
Haunted dark lairs waiting
To be exorcised. When the moon hung

Like a swinging lamp we stalked
Their entrances, judging distance,
Assessing the proper speed. John-John,

Lefty, Walt, Jughead, and me. Trained
In such matters we took off swift as Mercury
Darting through Hades. This was not like

Jumping off the roofs of abandoned
Buildings onto used mattresses.
We did not know what lurked behind

The tight narrow darkness; demons
& spooks trailing our footsteps. Terror
& thrill circled us like satellites.

Metal fences & brick walls housed
God-fearing dogs, howling at our torsos.
Like gunshots on New Year's Eve.

We bolted and dashed and stomped
Through trash: diapers, soda bottles,
Bread wrappers, dog shit. Wide-eyed,

Arms flailed like sperm tails, sweat
Dripped from our faces, our legs were horses.
The sound of hearts beating in a ship

Of wails. We heard field hollers.
Deliverance tickled our noses.
We escaped our own carcasses.

We became the wind, the stars, oceans
Inhabiting a space reserved for ancestors.
Locked in a rhythm of motion,

Catching up with time, running alongside
Our forefathers. Our bodies becoming
This home beating back drums.

Part Three

*

Don Pullen at The Zanzibar Blue Jazz Café

Half-past eight Don Pullen just arrived
from Yellow Springs. By his side
is the African-Brazilian Connection.
If it were any later, another space,
say "Up All Night Movie Hour"
on Channel 7, he might have been
a cartel leader snorting little mountains
of cocaine up his mutilated nostrils
from behind his bureau as he buries
a flurry of silver-headed bullets
into the chests of the good guys:
an armlock M-16 in his right hand,
a sawed-off double barrel shotgun
in his left, his dead blond
girlfriend oozing globules of blood
by the jacuzzi. No one could be cooler
balancing all those stimulants. No one.

She said she couldn't trust me,
that her ladybugs were mysteriously
disappearing, that I no longer
sprinkle rose petals in her bath,
that some other woman left a bouquet
of scented lingerie and a burning
candelabra on our doorstep, that she
was leaving, off to France—
the land of authentic lovers. In this club
the dim track lights reflecting off
the mirror where the bottles are lined
like a firing squad studying their targets

makes the ice, stacked on top of ice,
very sexy, surprisingly beautiful & this
is my burden, I see Beauty in everything,
everywhere. How can one cringe upon
hearing of a six-year-old boy snatched
from a mall outside of London, two
beggarly boys luring him to the train
tracks with a bag of popcorn only to beat
his head into a pulp of bad cabbage!
Even now, I can smell them
holding his hand promising
Candyland in all its stripes & chutes.

Nine-fifteen, Don & the African-
Brazilian have lit into Capoiera.
The berimbau string stings my eyes
already blurring cognac, my eyes
trying to half-see if that's my muse
sitting up front, unrecognizable,
a blue specter. Don's wire fingers are
scraping the ivory keys, off-
rhythm. It doesn't matter, the Connection
agrees there's room as they sway
& fall against the ceiling, a band
of white shadows wind-whipped
on a clothesline. Don's raspy hands—
more violent than a fusillade of autumn
leaves pin-wheeling like paper rain
over East River Drive in blazing reds
& yellows—hammers away, shivers in
monstrous anarchy. Don's arms arch like

orange slices squirting on my mouth's roof,
juice everywhere. His body swings up
off his haunches. The audience, surveying each
other's emotions, feel the extensions; their
bodies meld against the walls, leaving
a funeral of fingerprints as they exhale back
to their seats. Ten minutes to twelve,
I'm waving a taxi through holes
in the rain. I will tell her about tonight,
tell her how a guy named Don & his crew
The Connection hacked harmonies,
smashed scales, pulverized piano keys,
all in rhythm as each brutal chord
exploded in a moment's dawning.

Oregon Boogie

Khanum, the things we did,
that off-night at The Vet's
when Sister Sledge
issued from the jukebox's

lit dome the darker
rhythms of our native
homes; so, waiving all decorum
maps heap upon fugitives

our bodies made one nation
while in cold pints of pale ale
a couple broke conversation—
toasted our bacchanal.

Half-swaying, we met
& our lips splashed
like words over a page's white
shores, the foamy crash

of the lonely heart at work,
my hand coasting up
the valley in your back,
arriving at the nape thick

with ringlets I slowly brought
to face & inhaled as you spun
out, a laughing pirouette;
the desert in my heart was gone.

But, what of the province
beyond that empty dance floor,

the single-mindedness
of beating rain, the silent slurs

masked by cups of caffeine,
the half-hearted grins,
that say, *Here in Eugene*
it's not the color of your skin . . .

but all the while making
a fetish of progressiveness.
Along the Willamette,
consciousness thins out

like smoke rings of cannabis,
as the city dances the salsa,
as students sip cups of chai,
over bell & Cornel, as henna

designs flake from wrists.
The idea WE ARE FAMILY
finds its artificial ghost
in the circle of a spun Frisbee.

At The Vet's Club
your smile wide as a gorge;
others eventually joined
doing the "Eugene Dance,"

a spastic, organic whirling.
A break before the next song,
over the jukebox's neon
face, we leaned, waiting—
Bob Marley wailing!

Leaving Saturn

Sun Ra & His Year 2000 Myth Science Arkestra
at Grendel's Lair Cabaret, 1986

Skyrocketed—
My eyes dilate old
Copper pennies.
Effortlessly, I play

*

Manifesto of the One
Stringed Harp. Only
This time I'm washed
Ashore, shipwrecked

*

In Birmingham.
My black porcelain
Fingers, my sole
Possession. So I

*

Hammer out
Equations for
A New Thing.
Ogommetelli,

*

Ovid & Homer
Behind me, I toss
Apple peelings in
The air & half-hear

*

Brush strokes, the up
Kick of autumn
Leaves, the Arkestra
Laying down for
*

New dimensions.
I could be at Berkeley
Teaching a course—
Fixin's: How to Dress
*

Myth or Generations:
Spaceships in Harlem.
Instead, vibes from Chi-
Town, must be Fletcher's
*

Big Band Music—oh,
My brother, the wind—
I know this life is
Only a circus. I'm
*

Brushed aside: a naïf,
A charlatan, too avant-
Garde. Satellite music for
A futuristic tent, says
*

One critic. Heartbreak
In outer space, says
Another,—lunar
Dust on the brain.
*

I head to NewYork.
NewYork loves

A spectacle: wet pain
Of cement, sweet
*

Scent of gulls swirling
Between skyscrapers
So tall, looks like war.
If what I'm told is true,
*

Mars is dying, it's after
The end of the world.
So, here I am,
In Philadelphia,
*

Death's headquarters,
Here to save the cosmos,
Here to dance in a bed
Of living gravestones.

A Joyful Noise
Sun Ra & His Astro-Infinity Arkestra
at Slugs Saloon, 1968

I created a vacuum.
My story is a mystery.
Ain't no way they
Can fill a vacuum.

*

Never again will
They hurt me. All
I hear is death. You
Can only play what

*

You feel. So I butcher
The classics. I'm free.
I'm black. They call
It avant-garde.

*

I hate myself for being
In the position of playing
In a territory like this:
I didn't want to be

*

Here. They say history
Repeats. I'm gonna
Tell them 'bout their
Potential to bypass

*

Reality. I dream too
Much. I'm not there
As a woman. That's
Where I focus thoughts.

*

I have to hurt friends
For enemies. Because
Of my ideas. If you're
Going with a master

*

You have more
Options than
Going alone. I could
Be in Congress.

*

I did the equations.
I'm not where
I'm supposed to be.
I could be in college.

*

Two psychics told me.
They should have a holiday.
For musicians talk about
How beautiful. No Air.

*

No Light. No sound.
No Life. No Death.
No Energy. No
Nothing. I am full of

*

Hate tonight. They
Don't give me
A dime. They gonna hurt
Their very souls.

Crossing Over
Sun Ra & the American Spirit Arkestra
at the Fondation Maeght, 1970

Death, but not
A death. Half-wit
Minutes, homogeneous
Seconds, observed

With open arms,
The way myths end
& encircle you.
On a train to Nots,

I caught a glimpse;
It must have been
This way in Kush,
Amid the Pharaohs

Cork-bronzed eyes,
Airtight helmets,
Whose stone-bones
Served as vessels.

Mars? Venus?
Not the point!
What but a family
Of Dynasties endowed

With the divine
Cadence to administer
The infinite swells
& ripples of Funk?

What if the stream attains
The music? Does it mean
The end to responsorial
Calls, the shuck

& jive of briefcase
Men, the termination
Of Image Awards?
Or can one museum

Rhythm? Where is
Parker's horn?
In any event, we flaunt
The stuff of old

& modern hipness
As if it were a claim
Ticket. The day will
Come: we will have

Wished the world
Had CABBAGE PATCHED
With us, did the PREP
With as much mock

Capitalistic savvy,
PEE WEE HERMANED
Themselves into stiff
Bouts of kindness.

At moments, when we lose
Parts of ourselves,
Even if we know nothing
Of Legba, Oshun,

Obatala, we do know it
Has always been the case
To share the bopology.
How else to explain

A SOUL TRAIN line
Or the magic pull
Of THE ELECTRIC SLIDE,
So much better at willing

Conformity than the Bill
Of Rights? How else
To explain a people
Willing to groove

The Founding Fathers
Till they sweat abundantly
In nods, shuddering
Out of control.

Between Two Worlds
Sun Ra & His Solar Arkestra
at The Painted Bride Art Center, 1992

Galaxy gowns
& velveteen caps,
A pageant of black
Mummers, fire-eaters,

*

Flying afrobats.
In The Month of May
Arrival Zone USA.
Bongos, bamboo

*

Flutes, clavinettes.
We cross the stage
Like a rope of knotted
Elephants, shambling

*

Single file. Tonight's
Probe: Was God
An Astronaut? Sun
Harps, space drums,

*

Vibraphones. I dream
Of Saturn, my home
Moon, Phoebe, my last
Mission under

*

Different stars.
I strike the keyboard,
Prelude to Stargazers,
& recall that night
*

At Club de Lisa's,
1946, a party of white
Patrons pulling back
The curtain separating
*

The races. Sound
Scopes, Rocksichords,
Oboes. 5 billion
People on this earth
*

All out of tune.
Minutes from
The cracked bell
I plot a map
*

Of stars: Ursa Major
to Vine & 2nd & order
This gathering of
Intelligent earthlings
*

To embark upon tonight's
Spaceship—Ihnfinity, Inc.
Cosmic koras, bassoons,
Sharp, brass trumpets.
*

Beamed on
The cyclorama, Novas
Moons & Jupiter's
Baleful eye. Cow bells
*
Wind synths, organ
Music. My Myth
Space Lab, next best
Thing to a crystal ball.

Part Four

*

I'll Fly Away

I'm best when I'm running full-throated
towards the whitecaps in Truro,
piping my woeful tunes swell upon swell,
keeping company with the red-winged blackbird
who my ancient friend Gerry once said
governed these parts with his running mate,
the dusty miller. One ruled by land, the other
by sea; one painted the air with swoops
and trills and praised shafts of light,
the other buried himself in sand, imitating tyrants,
cursing the vast tongue of the ocean. This was years
before Henry James and the Mayflower
and the founding of the ballot and years before
Wm. Bradford established his ale house
on Main in Provincetown.

*

Today I run the shoreline with my neighbor's collie,
blessing his dumb search for wet bark
with a little jaunt of my own, exchanging
dirges of our common dream of flight,
my arms thrown back to lift my capelike towel,
thinking what would it have been like
if there had been no footprints to study
the way back to my beloved grief
if children had not waved my journey
through seaweed and spindrift
if I would have lived all day watching
schooners and barges edge toward Brooklyn,
sipping my sweet glass of tea, dozing off
from time to time, breaker foam lapping
at my tired black feet.

*

There was never a sound beside the sea
except one and that was my long sigh
the horseshoe crab heard as a whisper
and there was never a shadow sprawled
above Truro large as the one I cast
the retired governor saw as a crow.
Little Orville and little Wilbur Wright
must have jogged along a beach like this one,
enraged to find no fresh sand to
spike their imprints, and no sea air free
of brine or herring calls or mollusks
or jellyfish, and fallen down beside them,
grieving, as I have on occasion, waiting
for water to come in quietly.

Sandpaper

After Lisa Yuskavage

We keep coming back to her tits.
Pulpy pink, small as kernels of a corn.
The artist enslaves. A stroke of wit!

Notice her bound wrists; a masochist?
High art or soft porn?
We can't resist; we come back to her tits

And her nondescript face, full of zits;
Her bulging pot belly and skinny pale arms.
Someone whispers, "Sheer kitsch!"

Even her mountainous hips
And string-bean neck is enough to mourn,
Still we return to her tits.

One blue eye, knock-kneed, her mouth stripped,
Her broomlike hair sketched in a storm.
Slick wit. Potato zits. Viewer turned objectivist.

Though we try, we cannot quit;
We gape, tallying her deformities.
Yet, we come back to her tits;
We can't resist; we come back to her tits.

A Lesson after Swimming

1

PEACE-KEEPING

Gagged & fleeting,
a trumpeter's three-note riff—
kidnapped in the wing
flurry, an impulsive moment—
the gawky hand solos
of a mute drummer.
We ponder
the seasons of Father.

2

SUNDAY AFTERNOONS

Father is like a crossword puzzle,
each answer a clue.
The right words, a collection of spaces

harder to fill than a night
in New York City; the choices
innumerable & secret.

3

ELEGY

In a shirt tie, a boy swings;
His face painted white
By the lamp's upward stare.
Below is a book; its arms

Flapped wide-open.
Outside, his friends are
Calling. The Room is
Clean. The Lawn is cut.

4

SKYLINE

Thinks he's God. Soundless
as theory: the marriage
of skyscrapers & clouds,
that of God's cheekbones
& his machines.

God must be punch-drunk:
all those puny boxes splattering moonbeams
across a megagraphic screen,
shriveling an artist's paintbrush to
a meager keystroke.
He's triumphant.

5

MEMORY

I hear maracas
wrapped in cinnamon cloth
off the coast of Benin;
the sand, one dance
of desire

& vertical shapes
stringed by firelight
jerk their bodies

into mnemonic space.
Wooden masks adorn their face.

Benin is an embankment
of dreams & Father is
like a squatting chieftain,
with a cigar
between his rich, fat fingers.

Duck Girl on the Occasion of Spring

Everything in motion
  is about me. Azaleas
    & daffodils lunge swollen

heads skyward,
  each like a child peeping
    in a window:

the balustrade's promise
  of color like a lover's.
    In great numbers

old men sigh. Sharp blades
  of sunlight sparkle at Barclay,
    Savoy, & Liberty.

Only hours ago, Walnut Street
  was a canvas of footprints,
    men spoke & watched

their thoughts erupt
  in smoke. I am as still
    as a mountain. I evoke

a dance. Come closer.
  It appears as if I will swing
    this leg forward, twirl

my bronze toes. A wind
  rushes my thighs & sways

the folds in my chiton.

I hear the breathing
   of children tumbling
      in fresh grass. I wonder,

Do I live or am I dead?
   posed on this fish & swag
      base of limestone.

Where's my Pygmalion?
   my lover's eyes streaming
      in rain? I want to sprawl

beneath the bough
   of a black locust, buy
      time on one of the rows

& rows of settees, roller-blade
   around the square's
      perimeter, or like

the Philadelphia
   lawyer taking a break
      from being a Philadelphia

lawyer, pace the park
   till my pager calls me
      back to briefs;

thus the nature of my fate.
   Except for those years
      in the car-barn among

the rakes, ploughs, & hoes
I've been mired in the business
of beauty. How boring?

Not as much as The Lion
Crushing A Serpent. This Spring
Like every Spring, my wish—

an hour's worth of human
breath. I would let fly
this fowl & step a queen's

gracefulness or just once
let my hair down & dance
with the derelict who grabs

my stiff arm & does The Twist.
Spring! adorn me with
your green! Let foxgloves

burst & daylilies bloom
as I waltz silently
in the glare of your moon.

Called

My grandmother was out testifying
   at the big tent, and I stood
      in the arch of her bedroom

door, hoping to steal small
   change for a trip to Bullock's
      Corner Store where I would

empty my pockets and call out
   my favorite fare of goods:
      a pack of grape-flavored Now

& Laters, oatmeal cookies,
   three for a nickel, Mike & Ikes,
      Hot Tamales, a bag of fish.

Before the search I'd let
   a quiet mystery enter
      me, brushing my hands along

her mirrored dresser
   where lay a deck of funeral
      fans, Noxema cold cream,

postcards from Niagara,
   the upward splash
      of waterfall foam stilled

in a glittering sun. Then,
   like a lizard, I crawled
      on fours into her closet

& clambered over
an entrail of shoes strewn
about like slabs of granite.

In the distance, a glimmer.
I pulled aside the sheer,
drapelike gowns embroidered

with pearls & rhinestones,
made my way to a pink
patent-leather purse

which seemed to glow
like the bright head
of Jesus. When I flicked

the latch, it yawned,
revealing a fine cloth of silk
& a cellophane letter

from the great Billy Graham.
He said he wailed long
into the night, blessing

this cloth, no bigger
than a hankie, but of such
divine powers for only $15

it would bear forth
miracles rivaled only
by the Pope & his school

of saints. Imagine, a man
   of God shed tears
      so that a kid like me might

share the gift of healing.
   I went to the streets
      where I met Gladys,

the drunken cripple,
   whose left leg collapsed
      like a folding chair.

Saying nothing, I grabbed
   her knee & clung until
      our bodies shook,

until she bucked and fell
   on her back like a house
      roach. I ran further

and wrestled to the ground
   Champ, the three-legged cur,
      whose hop & roam hurt me

to watch. Clumps of dog-hair
   flew in my mouth as I whispered
      in his dog-ear some words

I had learned from the great
   Billy Graham: *Devil rebuke thee!*
      Then I swiped the air

where his hind limb should
　reappear! Still, I ran further
　　for there were many sinners

and found Adrienne who the kids
　teased for being retarded, for she
　　slobbered when she spoke

and couldn't wear her clothes
　straight. I threw my head back
　　as if to ask, *Is this the way,*

Lord? and grabbed her
　uncontrollable tongue.
　　Need I tell you it squirmed

in my hand like a pink fish
　out of water, holy and damp,
　　before I knew it a group of men,

whose faces I did not know,
　thrust me above their heads
　　while my body writhed

and I heard my name called
　over and over from somewhere deep—
　　Healer! Healer of All Things!

How to Listen

I am going to cock my head tonight like a dog
in front of McGlinchy's Tavern on Locust;
I am going to stand beside the man who works all day combing
his thatch of gray hair corkscrewed in every direction.
I am going to pay attention to our lives
unraveling between the forks of his fine-tooth comb.
For once, we won't talk about the end of the world
or Vietnam or his exquisite paper shoes.
For once, I am going to ignore the profanity and
the dancing and the jukebox so I can hear his head crackle
beneath the sky's stretch of faint stars.

Indian Song

Freddie Hubbard's playing the cassette deck
Forty miles outside Hays and I've looked at
This Kansas sunset for three hours now,
Almost bristling as big rigs bounce and grumble
Along I-70. At this speed cornfields come
In splotches, murky yellows and greens abutting
The road's shoulder, the flat wealth of the nation whirring by.
It's a kind of ornamentation I've gotten used to—
As in a dream. Espaliered against the sky's blazing—
Cloud-luffs cascade lacelike darkening whole fields.
30,000 feet above someone is buttering a muffin.
Someone stares at a SKYPHONE, and momentarily—
A baby cries in pressurized air. Through double-paned squares
Someone squints: fields crosshatched by asphalt-strips.
It is said Cézanne looked at a landscape so long he felt
As if his eyes were bleeding. No matter that. I'm heading west.
It's all so redolent, this wailing music, by my side—
You fingering fields of light, sunflowers over earth,
Miles traveled, a patchwork of good-byes.